Marie GAR

TOM-TI-RA

and the mysterious noise

Collins Educational

To my godchildren

Virginie

Bertille

and Matthieu

Knock, knock!

Knock, knock!

Knock, knock!

Knock, knock!

Knock, knock!

Knock, knock!

Mum!   Dad!

Knock, knock!

Knock, knock!

Knock, knock! Knock, knock!

Knock, knock!

Knock, knock!